Feelin' Good!
A Kid's Guide To Fort Lauderdale, FL

Photography by John D. Weigand
Poetry by Penelope Dyan

Bellissima Publishing, LLC
Jamul, California
www.bellissimapublishing.com

Copyright © 2017 by Penny D. Weigand and John D. Weigand

All rights reserved. No part of this book may be reproduced or transmitted in any form or by any means, electronic or mechanical, including photocopying, recording, or by any other means, or by any information or storage retrieval system, without permission from the publisher.

ISBN 978-1-61477-308-5
First Edition

"Follow the flamingos!"

Penelope Dyan

Feelin' Good!
Bellissima Publishing, LLC

Introduction

When you go to Fort Lauderdale, Florida, there is a lot to see and do. You can tour the everglades and go on an alligator hunt (with your eyes only, of course) or you can look for some flamingos on a Flamingo Gardens' tour. You can climb a tree. You can go shopping, or you can even go to the beach. The possibilities are endless!

Use this 'learn to read' book written by the award winning author, attorney and former teacher, Penelope Dyan, with photographs by John D. Weigand, to practice reading skills through the use of word recognition, word repetition and rhyme. The extra large print is perfect for young eyes, and the size of this book is perfect for a kid-sized backpack. See Fort Lauderdale through the eyes of a child, noticing the things only a child might see or notice.

When you are all finished reading this book, you can watch the free music video that goes with along with this book on Bellissimavideo's YouTube channel. Most of all, remember to have fun; because if a kid doesn't have fun learning, a kid won't love to learn. And also remember to listen for the songs of the places you visit, because all of life is one big song!

Feelin' Good!
Bellissima Publishing, LLC

Feelin' Good!
A Kid's Guide To Fort Lauderdale, FL

Photography by John D. Weigand
Poetry by Penelope Dyan

Fort Lauderdale, Florida is the city by the sea, where lots of fun waits for you and for me!

You can climb up a sideways tree,
IF you climb up CAREFULLY!
But don't climb up too fast!
And don't climb up too slow!
Even though
Mom WILL watch you from below.
Yes, Mom WILL be hovering there.
(It's safety first, after all.)
AND she WILL catch you
IF you start to fall!

You can also use your own two feet;
AND you can walk right down
this Fort Lauderdale, Florida street!

You can take a pedicab.
to go from here to there!
And here is one thing you will find. . .
they can take you everywhere!
They don't pedal too fast.
They won't pedal too slow.
And you can see all the sights,
as down the street you go!

You can see these sailboats,
one, two three!
(They really aren't meant
to sail the sea!)

Mom says,
"The beach is lovely!"
Dad says,
"I DON'T like gritty sand."
While Dad grumbles under his breath,
YOU think,
"I think THIS place is grand!"

Mom sees some pink flamingos
outside a seaside store.
You all decide to go inside,
where Mom is sure you will see more!

Then. . .
Mom nearly faints with fright,
as a giant great white shark
hangs down from the ceiling,
glowing in the light!

You see some yachts
in the seaside bay
And you think to yourself,
"Maybe I'll have one of those
someday!"

Back at your hotel
you swim and you play!
You think to yourself,
"I could do THIS all night,
AND I could do THIS all day!"

You get out of the pool.
You see two chairs
next to a game of giant chess.
Dad asks you,
"Who do YOU think plays THIS game?"
You tell him,
"I don't know . . .
some giants, I would guess!"

You ALL laugh, as ALL wrapped
up in beach towels (and wet)
you climb up the stairs to your room.
Mom sighs and says sadly,
"We will be going home soon."
And THAT thought
makes you feel KIND OF sad,
AND at the SAME time. . .
it makes you feel KIND OF glad!
Because as Dad points out,
"No matter how FAR you roam,
there REALLY is NO place like home!

"Home is where the heart is!"

A Proverb, Author Unknown

www.ingramcontent.com/pod-product-compliance
Ingram Content Group UK Ltd.
Pitfield, Milton Keynes, MK11 3LW, UK
UKHW060133240426

12048UKWH00002B/14